Wrinkled Missionaries

Wrinkled Missionaries

by
Phyllis Gunderson

Springville, Utah

ISBN: 1-55517-692-5
e.1

Published by CFI
Imprint of Cedar Fort Inc.
www.cedarfort.com

Distributed by:

Cover design by Nicole Cunningham
Cover design © 2003 by Lyle Mortimer

Printed in the United States of America
10 9 8 7 6 5 4 3 2 1

Library of Congress Cataloging-in-Publication Data

Gunderson, Phyllis.
 Wrinkled missionaries / by Phyllis Gunderson.
    p. cm.
 ISBN 1-55517-692-5 (pbk. : alk. paper)
 1. Mormon missionaries. 2. Mormon aged--Religious life. I. Title.
 BX8661.G86 2003
 266'.9332--dc21
                                        2003003526

Dedicated to mature missionaries who
give their golden years to God.

TABLE OF CONTENTS

INTRODUCTION

The call to teach English in Bangkok, Thailand as a charitable mission was unusual. Many of us hadn't considered a mission. We were recruited. The Church needed retired teachers who could show Thai teachers better ways to introduce English in their classrooms. There was no curriculum, no text, no way to evaluate. We landed with a thud and started running.

Eight couples and eight single sisters scattered themselves across Bangkok, a city of ten million people, to work with 15,000 English teachers in 429 primary schools. We were forbidden to preach the gospel in any form.

Our average age was seventy, with the usual aches of aging. Two of the sisters were seventy-seven. One man was eighty. I watched these dedicated people do an amazing job and realized there were other wrinkled missionaries across the world who were also doing an amazing job. Their stories and examples are worth telling.

This book begins in Thailand, but it doesn't end there.

Phyllis Gunderson

FOREWORD

by President Michael Goodman
Mission President, Thailand, 1996-1999

It is not possible to accurately put into words the contribution our senior missionaries made to the work in Thailand. Throughout my three years as a mission president, we had between 30 or 40 senior missionaries at any given time. They served for an average of one and a half years. Theirs was a work of pure charity that sent and will send ripples of influence through Thai society and the Church for generations to come. Thousands of people who might never have felt of the Savior's love received rich doses of it through these missionaries.

Couples and single sisters largely worked with a population our proselyting missionaries are hard-pressed to contact, the well educated and the professionals. These people often work long hours and are seldom available to our proselyting missionaries. They truly marveled at the selfless service given to them by our senior missionaries. They often asked, "what are you getting for your work?" and were dumbfounded to hear that the senior missionaries received nothing but the joy of serving. I had many tell me how amazed they were that these people would leave their homes and families and come all the way to Thailand just to "serve."

But their service was only part of the profound

influence these senior missionaries had on the Thais and the Lord's kingdom. They radiated such a sincere goodness that the Thais fell in love with them. Their sincerity, happiness, and gentle nature made them instantly part of the family. In fact, "mother," "father," "grandmother," and "grandfather" were not unusual titles with which the Thais referred to them. Truly, they touched thousands of lives in a profound way. For some Thais, this contact may be the only experience they will ever have with a Latter-day Saint. They will forever remember these "Latter-day Saints" as just that, Saints. Some were so impressed they have sought out members or others to tell them more about these unique people.

The service of senior missionaries has gone a long way to clearing up misunderstandings about Latter-day Saints that have existed for more than thirty years in Thailand. It was impossible for people who came in contact with these Christ-like missionaries to ever again believe misinformation that may have come their way. They were truly ambassadors for Christ in every sense of the word. They did things that, for all their efforts, the proselyting missionaries could never accomplish.

I consider it a singular blessing to have had the privilege of serving with these amazing brothers and sisters. Our mission and the country of Thailand has been forever blessed and changed by their service.

President Michael Goodman

WRINKLED MISSIONARIES

"They shall still bring forth fruit in old age; they shall be fat and flourishing."

Psalms 92:14

Young missionaries are like gold, glorious in their youth with skin stretched tight across their faces. They laugh in the wind as they ride bicycles across the world, preaching the gospel under the direction of God. Nobody does it better.

Wrinkled missionaries are like platinum, not as shiny, not as noticeable, but extremely rare and valuable. Mission Presidents clamor for them. They aren't just an added attraction, they are vital in opening doors to closed nations. Countries that sound like titles of fantasy novels welcome older couples and single sisters. There is a desperate need for the training, maturity, and experience offered by wrinkled missionaries. But, like platinum, senior missionaries are hard to get. The MTC has an average of only seventy older missionaries compared to 4,000 young ones. A ratio of 57:1 requires some answers.

At a mission reunion of mature couples and single sisters, one of the guests was a 60-year-old woman in good health with an equally healthy bank account. She listened to the adventures, admitted wistful admiration, but announced she could never do it.

"Why not?" someone asked.

"I'm not sure," she answered. "I guess I'm afraid."

"What are you afraid of?"

"I just..." she halted. "I don't want to live those rules. Up at the crack of dawn, in bed by nine, knocking on doors that slam in my face. I'm too old to go tracting, deal with rejection, or learn a foreign language. And I don't want to be supervised."

She couldn't be more wrong. The reality is, wrinkled missionaries are adults. Nobody supervises them because they don't need supervision. They get up at the crack of dawn and fall into bed at nine all by themselves. They manage their schedules and lives and do their magnificent best with the work they've been given.

But when they look in the mirror at a face with tissue paper eyes over sagging jowls, they sometimes ask themselves, "What am I doing? I'm giving precious time to go to the other side of the world where I can't drink the water, I shouldn't pet the dogs, and I'm leaving my grandchildren with my children. What am I doing!"

There are three possible answers:

1. A Proselyting Mission.

It isn't the same kind of mission the young missionaries are assigned. You don't have to tract unless you request it, there's no memorizing, and afternoon naps can be part of the schedule. Responsibilities include leadership training, member activation, convert fellowshipping, welfare service, visitor centers, community service, family history centers, and public relations.

2. A Service Mission.

Missionaries teach university classes in the fields of their training, repair school buildings, help refugees, work in orphanages, or teach English around the world. Assignments are tailored to the skills and training of the individual. From 1985-2001 there have been 7,205 projects in 147 countries, valued at $444 million.

3. A Temple Mission.

Missionaries serve wherever needed, as the temple president requests. This will primarily be ordinance work, but seniors could find themselves happily planting flowers every now and then.

A mission president put a nice little twist to the "What am I doing" question by saying, "Why am I doing?" With that simple grammar change, the answer becomes the same for everybody: "I'm doing this because the Lord needs me."

This volume of true stories is designed to answer the questions and concerns of seniors in the Church who don't realize how much they have to offer. The experiences of former wrinkled missionaries provide reassurance and courage. Others have left homes, families, and familiar surroundings to be scattered across the world. Furthermore, those same saints tend to turn around and do it again.

Nobody does it better.

THE $500 FULFILLMENT

"Verily, verily, I say unto you, even as you desire of me so it shall be unto you; and if you desire, you shall be the means of doing much good in this generation."

D&C 6:8

Lynn and Ray had a large family and managed a small business in a tiny eastern Utah town. When all their children left to create homes of their own, the bishop asked if they would consider going on a mission. Debts prevented them from accepting the call. Then Ray developed a cough that wouldn't go away. Seven months later he died of cancer.

Lynn found herself alone at the age of fifty-seven, owning a farm without animals, an old house full of furniture, a tire shop with an inventory of tires, a mountain of debts, and a friend willing to buy. She sold everything to pay the debts. When the dust settled, all she had in the world was a monthly $500 check from Ray's VA pension. Her bishop called her in for a talk.

"I promised Ray I'd take care of you," he said. "What can I do to help?"

"Well," she answered, "you could send me on that mission now."

The bishop grinned. Unlike couples, single sisters follow the same financial rules as the young missionaries; they pay $350 a month and the Church

5

picks up the rest. Lynn's pension would cover a proselyting mission. Three months later, she stepped off a plane into the London South Mission, where her son had served eighteen years earlier. "I'm so ignorant of the world," she said. "Everything I knew about England I'd learned from the movie *Mary Poppins*."

Lynn's mission increased her closeness to the Lord beyond her expectations. "It was the best thing that ever happened to me," she said. "I loved the people. I'm still in contact with investigators who never joined the Church and I'm still trying to get them to read the Book of Mormon I gave them."

After eighteen months of service, Lynn left England to return to her legal residence in America (the spare bedroom of her sister's house) and immediately submitted papers for her next mission. "It's so fun to get a surprise," she laughed. "That's the exciting part, when you get your papers and rip open that envelope. It was Thailand! Everything I knew about Thailand I'd learned from the movie *The King and I*."

"Thailand was an entirely different experience," Lynn explained. "I showed Thai teachers how to teach English to their students. I wanted to tell them about the Gospel, but I wasn't allowed to say a word on religion. I struggled with that rule while I fell in love with the people."

Since it was a humanitarian project, Thailand would cost Lynn $600 a month. Any mission besides proselyting, including humanitarian, temple, genealogy, family history, and visitor centers, is a self-pay program. Fortunately, Lynn had managed to save money during her service in England.

At the end of twenty months, she returned to the spare bedroom, deposited a few souvenirs in a box in the basement, visited her fourteen children and thirty-seven grandchildren, and made an appointment with the bishop.

"I'm back," she told him, "and I need new papers."

"Already?" he questioned.

"Absolutely," she said. "I need to get doctor and dentist physicals and all the signatures."

"Why do you want to be on a mission rather than just serving in the ward for awhile? You should take a break, and your sister would be glad to have you stay with her."

Lynn had to consider her answer. She didn't know a word strong enough to express how she felt but "fulfillment" seemed to come close. "The Church has done so much for me, I can't pay back enough," she said. "And I am fulfilled in serving the Lord through missions."

The call came to preach the Gospel in Russia.

When I visited Lynn at the Senior MTC in Provo, her small room was covered with scraps of paper bearing Russian words in the Cyrillic alphabet. Greek-looking symbols hung from drapes, walls, mirrors, and doors. She needed to speak Russian this time around. It was the first time language training had been necessary in her mission assignments.

Lynn is a beautiful woman in her sixties, attractively dressed, her thick gray hair in a stylish cut. To look at her, you'd never guess she has none of the material things so important to most of us.

"Don't you miss having a place to put your

treasures?" I asked. "Where do you keep all your things?"

"I don't need things," she said. "I don't have a home, car, or furniture, no china, pretty silver, or standard grandma memorabilia and my sister gathers my mail and pays my tithing for me."

Lynn told the story of a friend who went on a mission. It was a struggle to decide what to sell, what to keep, whether to rent out her house or not, and who would handle her debts and taxes while she was gone. "I'm totally free," explained Lynn. "I'm out of debt, have no decisions to make, and the IRS doesn't bother me. I couldn't live in America on my $500 pension, but it takes me around the world on missions."

"Do you have future plans?" I asked.

"I have good health. When I return, I'll send in my papers again and keep doing what I'm doing."

I left the Senior MTC, which Lynn considers her real home.

"I wish you the best," I said.

"Do svidanya," she replied, smiling.

The Russian was already kicking in.

LAUGHING IN
EVERY LANGUAGE

*"...and all nations feared greatly, so powerful was
the word of Enoch, and so great was the power of
the language which God had given him."*

Moses 7:13

A tall, brawny man with a mop of white hair
stood behind the podium and announced his inten-
tions. He and his wife were leaving the Senior MTC
for Armenia the next week and he was determined to
give the closing prayer in Armenian. All seventy
wrinkled missionaries in the audience, awed by his
courage, bowed their heads. Very few received
language training and even if they had, none were
willing to put the language where their mouth was.

The man stumbled over his first memorized
words like a baby tripping on his own toes. Every
utterance was agony, each syllable carefully chosen
and placed in the prayer where it belonged. Sweat
beaded on his forehead as he labored to express himself in the foreign language he tried to master. When
the prayer finished with a final "amen," (the only
recognizable word), the audience breathed an audible
sigh of relief. His wife dabbed at her tears. He had
said the prayer in Armenian, by golly. He did it!
Everyone laughed with him for the joy of it.

Most of us do a miserable job learning a
language. It's a primal fear for older people. Our

foreign-language-brain-cells have atrophied and it reminds us how vulnerable, how old, we've become. We tell a girl she's pretty, only to find we've called her bad luck. We bow to an elderly woman and pronounce "grandmother," then realize we've called her "grass." It's possible to say the stinking smell is good, the rice is a newspaper, and call yourself a banana. There's only one sane thing to do—laugh.

While we struggle with language, the young elders and sisters cut through it like butter and native speakers respond with comprehension. Soon a profound realization forms; the young missionaries need the language as part of their calling. It is vital to their work and the Spirit is with them. Mature missionaries are called to perform services ranging from humanitarian to health to English and everything in between. They receive inspiration for their assignment. A knowledge of the language often isn't necessary, even to get around town. Communication occurs with grins, groans, and gestures. When a taxi gets them where they need to be, even the driver cheers while everybody laughs.

In the tiny foreign branches of the Church, sometimes so small they should be called twigs, older missionaries feel the sweet sincerity of the members without understanding their words. They join a struggling ward choir where the LDS hymnbook looks like it's written in Sanskrit. There's no way to read the stuff, so they sing with all their hearts "watermelon, watermelon" to the tune of "Joy to the World." It's a time-honored way to fake words, but the choir director says, (as the Elders interpret) "If you can't learn the song in the correct language, you should sing it in English." They laugh.

A couple found themselves in Russia, where they attended Sacrament Meeting wrapped in heavy coats, sitting on cold, hard benches. When the announcements were made (in Russian, of course) the good brother heard what he thought was his own name. Not wishing to appear ignorant, he raised his hand with the rest. "Did you understand that?" he whispered to his wife. She grinned wickedly at him and replied, "I think you've just been made a Sunday School teacher in a Russian-speaking branch of the Church." The befuddled man considered the difficulty of the assignment. Fortunately, one of the young Elders informed him that he had been sustained as First Counselor in the Branch Presidency. But if the call had been a Sunday School class, he was ready to do his best.

"So...," friends ask when mature missionaries return from a foreign country, "did you learn the language?" The question is difficult because "I tried" doesn't count. It's like saying to a mountain climber, "So...did you make it to the top?" If the answer isn't "yes," there's no good answer. So wrinkled missionaries respond with, "Yes, I learned the language, but nobody learned to understand me."

The couple who went to Armenia needed to speak Armenian and the spirit rested on their language efforts. An elderly sister, called to teach seminary in Mexico, learned Spanish. Couples in Yekaterinburg speak Russian as they work among the people, loving both the people and their language. But most mature couples and sisters are called to places where the only communication skills needed are a smile and a laugh.

Everybody laughs in the same language.

THE TOILET TESTAMENT

"And thus we see that by small means the Lord can bring about great things."

1 *Nephi 16:29*

Sydney and Dawn arrived in Vientiene, Laos expecting a city. There wasn't one. "It was made up of many little villages connected by dirt roads," Dawn said. "A beer company is the largest business in Laos, with Pepsi Cola running a close second."

Eighty-five percent of the people in Laos are rural. They weave, sew, grow rice, eat weeds, and raise a pig and some chickens. Diarrhea is the number one health problem. And 72-year-old Sydney had been called as the Country Director to preside over four couples.

That was it.

To serve the whole country.

Four couples.

Laos, of course, was thrilled to get them and begged for more. Wrinkled missionaries are welcomed, in demand, appreciated, and bargained for. But there weren't any more. Elder Sydney had his fair share.

They began teaching English at the School of Health Technology in Vientiene, a small college of about 700 students. From that base they commenced the heart and soul of their calling, Charity, the pure love of Christ. The Church sent school supplies for the

13

couples to distribute and hundreds of bags found their way to eager little hands that reached for paper, pencils, crayons, and pictures. During one of these hand-out sessions, Sydney and Dawn noticed something vital was missing at the school...there weren't any bathrooms. No toilets. They surveyed the flat surface of the land and realized the lack of even a decent-sized bush. So, as indelicate as the subject seemed to be, they asked the principal. Sure enough, there were no toilets. One of the side effects of such a lack was that the older girls stopped coming to school. "It is a sad shame," the principal lamented, "but what can I do?"

Sidney and Dawn knew what they could do. Latter-Day-Saint Charities allowed them to sponsor small projects of $1,000 each and this looked perfect. Arrangements were made with proper Laotian authorities. The Area Welfare Agent in Hong Kong authorized a thousand dollars to purchase bricks, mortar, roofing, tile, and three little ceramic bowls to fit nicely into holes dug for the purpose. Teachers, parents, and villagers supplied the labor. Work was slow but sweet.

In the meantime, a student at the college heard about the toilet project and approached them. "The school in my district has also no toilets," he said. "We would ask if you help us." Elder Sydney wrote the required papers, contacted the appropriate authorities, and the next thousand dollars arrived within days. "In a month they had it done," Sydney smiled at the memory. "The construction wasn't smooth, but it worked!"

A celebration honoring the six new toilets

attracted local news coverage. Praise and flowers were profuse, lights flashed, cameras whirred, and the couple participated in the "opening ceremony" by handing over the key to the...uh...toilets. A plaque in their honor still graces the wall.

After that, projects "washroomed" and the couple found themselves knee-deep in commodes. Some facilities were well-designed septic tanks with a tower to deliver water, while others were little more than outhouses. But the villagers designed and built them with pride.

A variety of thousand-dollar causes blossomed while the original projects continued. They remodeled the college canteen, furnished English textbooks for the Ministry of Education, and replaced rough, unpainted wooden chalkboards. They sponsored the construction of a bridge across the Mekong River to an island serving as home for three hundred people. Since the flood season usually stranded the islanders, the quarter-mile bridge was approved and appreciated.

"Project Garbage Can" was born when one of the missionary couples picked up trash during a walk and couldn't find a place to deposit it. The result was a proposal which supplied thirty garbage cans throughout Vientiene. Two very small garbage sorting centers were built so the beer and Pepsi cans could be recycled.

It didn't take long for Sydney and Dawn to notice that many farmers used sticks as implements in their work. They contacted city officials to ask if they could supply tools. "Even the village heads had to be contacted before we would consider any project,"

Sydney explained. They bought tools made in Thailand at a Chinese hardware store and, for a thousand dollars, nine villages were supplied with good shovels, picks, rakes, hoes, hammers, and saws.

In a related farming project, the wrinkled missionaries bought a two-wheel hand tractor for an isolated village in the northern mountains of Laos. The couples smiled as they imagined villagers craning their necks and shading their eyes when the new tractor arrived by helicopter. The small tractor would increase production from four hectares to twenty hectares.

During their missionary service, Sydney, Dawn, and their small band of wrinkled missionaries averaged a humanitarian project each month, in addition to teaching English at the college. The toilet undertaking alone benefited seven hundred children and the older girls started attending school again. Not bad for a bunch of old folks in their seventies.

After one year at home, Sydney and Dawn answered a call to return to Laos.

WE LOVED OUR COMPANIONS. WE HATED OUR COMPANIONS.

"And he shall go forth in the power of my Spirit, preaching my gospel, two by two..."

D&C 42:6

"Where do we turn?" he says.

"I'm looking, I'm looking!" She scans the map.

"If we miss the turn-off, there's no way back for miles!"

She raises her voice to match his. "I'm doing the best I can! I think this map is wrong."

The Country Director, pressed on all sides by harried, honking traffic, steals a look at his wife. Her hair has wilted in the heat. She had stopped wearing makeup months ago because it melted. "Oh, NO," he shouts, "you've got the map upside-down!"

"Look, I can't read these squiggles!" she retorts. "Drive over in the left-hand lane so we can get off and figure it out." Left lane. The traffic pattern is backwards. "Left lane! Left lane!" she shouts. It's insane to drive in Asia. They should have taken a taxi and been done with it. She tells him so. "Here's an exit!"

He glances in the rear-view mirror to see a stream of cars, buses, and taxis barreling toward his back bumper. He's in the wrong car on the wrong road

17

with the wrong map and (he suspects) the wrong wife.

"If our marriage survives this mission, we'll be a strong couple," she laughs when the worst is over.

Ideally, we expect our companions to be loving, kind, considerate, and Christ-like. When couples agree to serve a mission, it seems obvious their knowledge of each other and their experience raising a family has prepared them for 24/7 togetherness. The single sisters, trained in cooperation and charity through years of Relief Society activity, are expected to be angels by design. But reality raises its Medusa head. Couples often enter a mission as near strangers. They haven't spent an hour a day together for twenty years. The single sisters also have the difficult challenge to love a total stranger who offers daily introductions of nuances and quirks, reducing even the strongest woman to tears. We are human, and a mission provides the entire spectrum of human experience crushed into a miniature time frame.

Even Paul and Barnabas had companionship problems. After finishing a mission to the gentiles and organizing Christian headquarters in Antioch, they decided to return to Asia to check their converts. Barnabas invited a kinsman, Mark, to go along, but Paul was harboring a grudge against Mark from a previous mission experience and refused to take him. Barnabas didn't appreciate the unforgiving attitude toward his kinsman. Acts 15:39 records the result: "And the contention was so sharp between them, that they departed asunder one from the other; and so Barnabas took Mark, and sailed unto Cyprus; and Paul chose Silas, and departed..."

It happens to the best of us. These were the finest men of the Church. Paul, staunch and unyielding in the faith, willing to die for the cause. Barnabas, highly favored of the Apostles, fellow laborer and companion. Mark, writer of the second Gospel in the New Testament. But their human feelings exploded against one another and they separated. A mission is the best of times and the worst of times. We love our companions. We hate our companions.

Years later, as Paul waited for his execution in Rome, he sent a letter to Timothy requesting that Mark be brought to him, "...for he is profitable unto me for the ministry," he wrote. (2 Tim. 4:11) The rift had been repaired.

✤

George and Jean opened their mission envelope with traditional excitement. They knew it would be in the states because they had specified a one-year time limit, English only. The words "Kirtland, Ohio, Family History" hung in the air and made their commitment a fact. They received training at the Senior MTC and woke up a few weeks later in their new environment.

"He'd been retired for six months before we went on the mission," Jean said. "We hadn't spent a lot of time together for years. He worked, I raised children. It was a new experience to spend twenty-four hours a day together."

George was a leader, a planner, an organizer, and a speaker. He did it well and he did it alone. His wife was left with short scripture readings. She took the assignment and quietly smoldered.

As every missionary knows, the Spirit withdraws at even an invisible thread of bad feeling and the couple lost their most valuable ally. Even though they followed the rules, read the scriptures, and prayed, they struggled through three months of pushing and pulling through the mire of a mission without the help of the Holy Ghost. "The mission was nothing but drudgery," Jean admitted. Then one day, her frustration spilled out.

"I know as much about this as you do," she complained. "I have as many good ideas as you. I didn't come on this mission to be a tag-along."

Poor George had felt the tension, of course, and was vaguely aware that the Spirit was gone, but he couldn't connect it with himself in any way, so he had brushed his feelings aside. Now he stood there with mouth open as his quiet, shy little wife flooded him with anger.

"Unless I'm a full partner and companion," she demanded, "I'm staying at the apartment and you can go to the meetings alone."

In ordinary civilian life, the good brother would have left the house feeling betrayed and misunderstood. He was carrying the burden of their assignment and she showed no appreciation. But he couldn't go to the meetings alone. Missionaries teach as a couple. The unidentified conflict had to be resolved.

"Why didn't you speak up before?" he asked. "I always wanted you to do more."

A turned corner. A new leaf. The mission was executed and completed as a team. Afterwards, Jean explained, "It was one of the choicest experiences of our lives. The Spirit is so strong on a mission, it's unbearable to lose it. You do whatever is necessary to get it back. And we brought that awareness home with us."

George and Jean are sensitive now if the Spirit is lacking in their lives. They're still learning, and sometimes they forget, but when there's conflict in the marriage they look at each other and say, "What's wrong? What do we need to do?"

Two years after their return from Ohio, they submitted mission papers again, this time for eighteen months. "We learned from our first experience that we needed a year and half," they explained. "By the time you get there, find your way around, and learn your responsibilities, there's only a few months left. We needed more time."

George and Jean opened the mission envelope containing their new assignment with traditional excitement. The words "proselyting, Ireland" hung in the air and made their commitment a fact.

THE COUPLE
IN THE CUBICLE

"...why should I desire more than to perform the work to which I have been called?"

Alma 29:6

They were disappointed in the assignment. "We were expecting to make a difference in the world," Barbara said, "and here we are, pushing papers!" From early morning until late afternoon, they filled their call as the office couple in Bangkok, Thailand, staring at computer screens, documents, notes, and drafts. At the end of each day they returned to their Thai-style townhouse, exhausted and frustrated. They'd gone to the other side of the world to be isolated in a cubicle, watching others travel the country, hearing stories others had to tell. While the majority of couple missionaries taught English and toured the exotic Asian sights, Barbara and Nolan ground out nits and bits and money problems.

In a couple of months they had become accustomed to bottled water, a bed slightly harder than the floor, the fifty-two stairs that led to their office, and geckos chirping on the walls. They could bargain with Bahts and direct taxi drivers to the center of Bangkok, but they couldn't overcome their disappointment in the call to the cubicle.

Then, on an ordinary Sunday, they noticed three Asians sitting alone at the back of the chapel in the

English-speaking ward. Nolan and Barbara introduced themselves and it was love at first sight. One of the newcomers spoke enough English to tell the couple that they were Cambodian refugees. Every Sunday the couple from the cubicle sat by the refugees, eventually offering to teach a class in the cultural hall while Sumorn, the English speaker, translated. Each Sunday saw new investigators, legal refugees assisted by the United Nations humanitarian organization.

Nolan and Barbara had heard about refugees but now they experienced them as real people, with stories of pain and loss. A woman escaped with others of her village by swimming across the river at night, but her baby woke and cried. The mother held her baby underwater to protect the entire group and the child drowned. Two brothers, separated from their parents as children, never saw their family again. One man spent nineteen years in a Cambodian prison, kept alive only by faith that some unknown good existed in his future. The day he was baptized, he gave testimony in his native language that he had survived so he could find the gospel.

The couple invited their Cambodians to dinner. Barbara said, "When nineteen people came into our small, two-story townhouse they were wide-eyed. They asked how many families lived in the apartment. We told them just the two of us. Then they looked up at the second story and asked how many lived upstairs." The couple's cubicle was expanding.

Occasionally one of the refugees would say, "You are good cook, mother."

"Thank you," she would reply.

"What time you make food?"

"About six o'clock."

"Thank you. We come." They did and Barbara and Nolan were happy. Their guests were fond of the "little round green things" (peas), but not apple pie.

Finally the day came when the Cambodians were able to return a dinner invitation. The couple learned that refugees from eight different countries lived in one small apartment complex. "They served dinner outside," said Barbara, "on old boards instead of tables, with trees over our heads, roots at our feet, and absolute love. We knew they had saved a long time to buy the food. We dined with royalty that day."

Work in the cubicle droned on but their hearts were lighter. One Sunday, a Cambodian teenager stood in the hall. Barbara asked if he wanted to come to class with the other refugees. "We're going to teach about the temple," she explained.

"Oh, I already know about that."

"Really?" Barbara wondered what he'd heard. "What do you know?" she asked.

The boy replied in adequate English, "When I die, you will take my body to Salt Lake temple and work on it."

"You'd better come with me to class," laughed Barbara.

As the two of them walked arm in arm down the hall, she noticed the boy's badly twisted leg which forced him to move sideways. His name was Sophea and he had suffered polio as a child. His family was too poor to get help.

Nolan and Barbara worked in their cubicle and discussed Sophea, wondering if surgery could correct the boy's handicap. They took him to doctors, researched surgical procedures, wrote letters, and began the process of raising money. A series of surgeries took place over the next year, paid for by donations, welfare funds, and fast offerings from members of the Church of Jesus Christ of Latter-day Saints. The week before Nolan and Barbara were scheduled to leave Thailand, they took Sophea to have his final cast removed. "It was one of the sweetest moments of the mission," they said. Sophea's leg was as thin as Nolan's wrist, but it was straight! As they walked out of the office, Sophea, with tears in his eyes, said, "Look! My feet go in same direction!"

Two years later, at the age of eighteen, Sophea submitted his mission papers.

A boy can walk again because an office couple reached out to make a difference. Twenty-five Cambodian refugees are members of the Church because somebody cared enough to love them, and the new members are bringing in others. Furthermore, Nolan and Barbara did the assignments vital to the operation of the mission, thereby freeing up two young Elders to preach the gospel. There was no longer disappointment at their calling to the cubicle. Their last letter home described how they felt:

"We're all packed and ready but really want time to stand still. How can we leave these people? We came to feed and instead we have been fed. Our hearts are full. Our lives will never be the same."

God knows what He's doing, even in a call to a cubicle.

AND SHOULD WE DIE...

"I have fought a good fight, I have finished my course, I have kept the faith."

2 Timothy 4:7

We don't know the purposes of God. It is sufficient to know that God knows. The entire truth may not be revealed for a very long time. One classic tale of missionary deaths with a future purpose is the following:

Palestine, 1890

Adolph Haag left Payson, Utah early in the 1890's to preach the gospel in Palestine. He was zealous in bringing Christ once again to the Holy Land, but Adolph sickened and died in 1892. He was buried in a cemetery in Haifa, a six-foot pillar marked the spot, the top broken off to symbolize a life cut short.

Alexander Clark arrived shortly after, contracted smallpox, and died in 1895. He was buried fifteen feet from Elder Haag, the top of his gravestone also broken by design. They were young men on an errand of the Lord, working with faith and diligence in preparation for the second coming, yet they died. Their bodies couldn't even be shipped home, but had to be placed in an obscure area north of Jerusalem. Where was God?

For nearly a century, the young men rested in their graves. Palestine went through upheaval, political intrigue, and wars. Then, during a relatively peaceful moment, the Church asked permission to build a center for semester abroad students. The request was denied. Jewish law required that the presence of a church be physically evident for several decades before permission to build in Jerusalem could be granted. The Church of Jesus Christ of Latter-day Saints was a very new religion.

Jerusalem officials were invited to the overgrown cemetery in Haifa to see the graves of Adolph and Alexander, the faintly etched writing on the stones still readable. The graves provided proof that the Church had been physically present before the turn of the century. Permission to build was granted.

The BYU Jerusalem Center was constructed prominently next to the Mount of Olives and attracted 70,000 tourists a year. Advertising wasn't necessary. Both Jews and Arabs called it the "Mormon University" and included it on tour agendas. The Jerusalem Center introduced the gospel without preaching a word. Adolph and Alexander reached more people in death than would have been possible in one lifetime.

Thailand, 2000

Dale and Helen had already served eighteen months but extended their mission until another couple could be recruited. They found themselves alone in northern Thailand on Dale's seventy-second birthday. What better place to be than on the other side of the world, serving the Lord? Dale said it was a great birthday, he'd never felt better or happier.

Helen slept lightly that night, so she was aware when Dale took a deep breath of air...and didn't exhale. She waited expectantly, then raised up to look at him. There was no noise, no movement, no breathing. She shook him. No response. A tidal wave of realization swept over her, Dale was gone.

Helen tried CPR but it didn't take long for her to know it was useless. Then came a calm assurance that the gospel is true. She knelt by him, took him in her arms, and talked to him. "I know you're here, Dale," she said. "I've told you this before, but I want to say it one last time before we meet again. I love you. Thank you for being a good man. Thank you for choosing me such a long time ago. It's been my blessing to be your wife." She told him she knew he was close by, but also understood he'd have to leave soon. "Please stay as long as you can," she said, "to help me through this."

A phone number came into her mind which belonged to a couple who were members of the Church, working for the U.S. government not far away. They'd had dinner together a while back, but there was no reason for Helen to remember their number. It simply appeared, stamped on her memory. She called the couple.

After that, everything became a cloud of unreality. She received a blessing and slept. The next morning, Helen rolled to her knees for morning prayer. Still in a fog of sleep, she held out her hand for Dale to take. It was a forty-year tradition. Then, as she remembered the night before, she felt his large, warm hand cover hers. His presence stayed with her throughout the packing, preparations, red tape, and flight back to America. His calm influence sustained her during the funeral. Then, Dale went home. Two years later, Helen served as a single sister in Romania.

We don't know the purposes of God. It is sufficient to know that God knows.

THE SEVEN MIRACLES OF A MATURE SINGLE SISTER

"Who can find a virtuous woman? For her price is far above rubies."

Proverbs 31:10

General Conference was almost the same as always. Joyce noticed a chill in the October air as children and grandchildren sprawled around the television. Food for her family waited while everyone feasted spiritually on the words of President Gordon B. Hinckley. Only one thing was missing this year; Joyce's husband. She knew the separation of death was temporary, thanks to the gospel, but five months hadn't been enough time to heal the pain. There was a hole in her soul and she'd need a miracle to heal it.

A knock on the door brought Joyce's sister-in-law, Virginia, to join the family feast. Virginia had recently submitted mission papers and been called on a CES (Church Educational Services) mission to Fiji, but a companion had not yet been found and the wait was getting on her nerves. "I'm frustrated," she said. "They can't find anyone to go with me." From somewhere out of the air, Joyce heard a voice declare, "I'll go with you." Apparently, she wasn't the only one who heard the mysterious voice, because a chorus of protests came from her children at the table. "Mother!" they gasped, "Do you know what you're saying?" Joyce looked around, a little stunned. She

31

wasn't absolutely sure she'd said it.

The unidentified voice was the first miracle.

Joyce's obstacles, her teaching contract, family obligations, and church responsibilities melted to clear a path for service. Two months later, Joyce and Virginia stepped off the plane in Suva, Fiji. Their assignment was to teach scriptures in a Primary School to 600 students who ranged in age from kindergarten through seventh grade.

The children's English skills were poor; they lacked even readiness for reading. Joyce asked her country director if he would consider providing a good foundation for English language skills at the kindergarten level. She wrote a curriculum, which was approved in Salt Lake, and initiated the first kindergarten program in Fiji. "That was the second miracle," she said. "The third miracle was when the Ministry of Fiji came to observe an in-service lesson. They wanted more information about raising the standards of the country."

"And the fourth miracle?" I asked.

"When the Church sent us a laminating machine!" she declared.

The fifth miracle was the production of the Church Bicentennial program, accomplished in less than four weeks. Every parent came, even though it was a rainy night. Joyce's students performed to a standing-room only crowd.

The next miracle took slightly longer.

Joyce and Virginia lived in the middle flat of a house full of widows. On the bottom floor lived a widow from India with two daughters and a son. The top floor housed another Indian family, a widow and her daughter. Both families were related, sisters and cousins. Joyce often watched the two sisters put trays of fruit on their heads to carry to the Hindu temple. Pleasantries and histories were exchanged and the single women formed a kind of "widow alliance."

One day, during an ordinary conversation, Joyce said, "Where do you think your husbands are? What do you think they're doing?"

"They're just dead," the women replied. "They might come back as a cat or dog or another person...we don't know."

"I'd like to tell you what my husband is doing," Joyce offered. "My husband is a missionary in the Spirit World, doing what I'm doing. Perhaps he is teaching important things to your husbands so they can have a happy forever-after."

The Indian women were astounded by the doctrine.

"If you'd like to know more," Joyce continued, "I know some young men you can meet with."

Joyce and Virginia hosted missionary discussions in their flat twice a week. They invited the family to Sunday meetings and socials. The women learned how to pray. They gave up coffee.

Shobit, the daughter who lived in the downstairs flat, committed to be baptized. The week before the scheduled event she had an amazing dream. Her father and her uncle, both dead, appeared to her dressed in white. "Shobit," they said, "you are doing the right thing. We are here waiting, reading the scriptures, wanting to learn more."

Shobit was baptized.

So was her mother, sister, brother, and cousin.

It was the sixth miracle.

I asked Joyce what the seventh miracle had been. Her eyes sparkled. "The Prophet came!" she said. "The Prophet came to Fiji."

Joyce's miracle mission was completed with honor. Two years in Fiji had given her what she termed a "treasure box." "I have a treasure box in my heart from this experience," she said. "The pearl of great price is the gospel. The wonderful members of the Church are my diamonds, refined and polished by the Church. I had many encounters with pure, faithful women and was reminded of Proverbs 31:10 'Who can find a virtuous woman? For her price is far above rubies.' They are my rubies. The beauty of the island and the sea that surrounds it are brilliant blue sapphires, treasures of my heart."

After a year at home, Joyce felt she needed more. "I had such a satisfying experience in Fiji," she said, "I wanted to do something again. I wrote on my mission papers that I was willing to go anywhere, but hoped I could go back to Fiji." They sent her to Thailand to teach English. Before the year was over, she was teaching at a prestigious television station, influencing her students to play the Tabernacle Choir on the radio. In another few months she was invited to teach English at the Parliament building in Bangkok. Her efforts helped open doors for the Church in a country that has not been friendly in the past.

After a year at home, Joyce applied for yet another mission. "I wrote on my mission papers that I was willing to go anywhere," she said. "But I was hoping to go back to Thailand." They sent her to Myanmar

(Burma). After three months in the country she sent an open e-mail to everyone on her list: "We truly need another couple here to share all the doors of opportunity that are opening up. It is an exciting time. People of great influence are asking for our assistance! Is anyone listening?"

While Joyce's miracles continue, we stand back to see the real miracle; Joyce herself.

CALL OF THE WILD

"I'll go where you want me to go, dear Lord. Except..."

Throughout the Church, the story is told of the little boy who dreamed of a mission to Japan, the land of his birth, the land of his ancestors, the country his parents had left when they joined the Church of Jesus Christ of Latter-day Saints. From his home in New York he had learned both the gospel and the Japanese language in preparation for his mission.

When the time came to open the envelope containing his call, he stared down at the words "South America." "There's been a mistake," he said. He wrote polite letters to the proper authorities requesting a review. The reply back said, "You have been given the correct assignment." He continued writing letters from the MTC about the mix-up. He had trouble concentrating on Spanish since he was sure he'd be re-assigned to Japan at the last minute.

In Columbia, he obediently followed his senior companion, but firmly believed someone would recognize the mistake and transfer him where he belonged. Twenty-two months slipped by and the Elder who should have gone to Japan was still in Columbia, still couldn't speak Spanish, and still served as a junior companion. With only two months of his mission left, he reluctantly realized his dream would not come true.

One day an Asian gentleman approached the two elders on the street and greeted them in Japanese. During the ensuing conversation, the two missionaries were invited to speak at a religious study meeting with the older gentleman, his family, and friends. When the young missionaries entered the room, sixty-four Japanese people stood to welcome them. The book they were studying was old and tattered, but it could still be identified as a Japanese Book of Mormon. They had been learning the gospel on their own and didn't know the next step. During the last few weeks of his mission, the misplaced Elder in Colombia finally did what he knew he was meant to do, he taught the gospel in Japanese and baptized all his contacts.

Mark and Cheryl lived in California. When they were called to Russia, they didn't know how to prepare. Even the summers in Russia are colder than the winters in California. The couple figured (along with a lot of missionaries) that the Brethren have a huge map on a wall and they throw random darts at it to determine who goes where. Nothing else makes sense. Unless (dare we say it?) God knows what He's doing.

Mark and Cheryl enjoyed their mission in Russia so much they immediately signed up again, requesting a return to Russia. Instead, they spent eighteen months as Country Directors in Asia. At the end of their service they received their next call, Mission President in Russia. The cold, the snow, the summers like winters, the politics, the language, nothing was an obstacle. God had prepared them.

Barbara had told the Lord she would serve Him anywhere He wanted her to go. "Except where it's hot," she said. "I can't stand the heat. I pass out." Nobody was listening. She was sent where she was needed, a hot country with air conditioning. She learned to stand in the shade. "Well," Barbara grinned, "the Lord knew what He wanted for me a lot better than I did."

Marge was called to England, a country she loved. To prepare, she happily collected wool skirts and read English history. But at the Senior MTC she was advised that her services were required on the opposite side of the world, in a place where she wouldn't be wearing wool and her English history was wasted. She quickly did an about-face, gathered a few cotton things, and went where the need was greatest.

If you don't get what you want, you most certainly will get what you need.

LIONS AND TIGERS AND BEARS, OH MY!

"And in that day the enmity of man, and the enmity of beasts, yea, the enmity of all flesh, shall cease from before my face.

D&C 101:26

The newest single sisters opened the door to their apartment. It seemed apparent their service mission on the other side of the world would start by cleaning up their own tiny living quarters. Cobwebs hung from corners in light brown shrouds. Dust covered everything, even though the city streets were five stories below. When they opened the door to one of the bedrooms, a quick movement on the wall caught their eye. It was a gecko, a lizard with suction cups that moves rapidly across walls and ceilings. They'd been told the creature was harmless, but still, it was unnerving.

The apartment contract had guaranteed a kitchen, two bedrooms, two beds, and an American toilet. Sure enough, it was all there as promised. There were two beds all right, but only one mattress. So the spry little ladies went into the streets and bought a new mattress, still crated in cardboard, and took it back to the apartment. When they ripped open the cardboard seams, two dozen cockroaches scattered across the floor, their armored bodies zigzagging like bumper cars at an amusement park. The sisters squealed as

41

they performed a dance of death, stomping, hitting, squishing, and crunching.

Cleanliness of the apartment would become vital in keeping control of the local bugs. There would be no spills, no open containers. All fruits and vegetables would be soaked in a cleansing solution. It was no big deal. The plucky women settled into a comfortable routine.

Then one day they saw what looked like a black, jagged crack in the wall...and it was moving. Closer inspection proved the crack to be an army of tiny ants marching doggedly across their wall. A spritz of ant poison quickly dropped the creatures, but others took their place to create a new trail. More ant spray, more dead ants, more living ones on the march to some destination.

"Where are they coming from?'

"Especially five stories from the ground!"

These were women who had married, raised children, lost husbands through both death and divorce, experienced broken legs, broken hearts, and survived. They discussed the problem, analyzed possibilities, and realized that a universe of ants lived in the walls of the complex. The sisters would asphyxiate themselves before they could poison all the ants. So they wisely decided to let the small creatures march in their happy formations. Live and let live! The geckos on the walls were given pet names. These were God's creatures. (O.K., all except the cockroaches.)

Animals and bugs in all their varieties are items on the "fear list" of potential wrinkled missionaries. Florescent green lizards found in the refrigerator, snakes on the front porch, and cockroaches everywhere, are stories that become legends. What should a helpless old person do?

The best advice is, don't worry about little things.

The absolutely worst danger/inconvenience/misery you will face on any mission anywhere in the world is mosquitoes. They can infect you with fatal viruses, administer welts that leave scars, and reduce you to a quivering, whining blob. You can be chased out of bed by a dive-bombing squadron of mosquitoes and hide in the bathroom to sleep on wet tile all night. Mosquitoes will quietly dine between your toes and have you squirming for days. For every cockroach that scurries across your floor, there will be a thousand mosquitoes clambering for their turn at the bite. A rampaging herd of elephants will make noise so you can get away. Mosquitoes attack without warning. Indeed, you don't know they've attacked until it's too late.

Experiment with a safe mosquito repellent before you leave home. A mosquito net for your bed will allow you to giggle when the enemy crawls around trying to find a hole. The net will be your lifeline to sanity, so take care of it. Let the lions and tigers and bears take care of themselves.

THE MYTH
OF THE EMPTY NEST

"I have no greater joy than to hear that my children walk in truth."

3 John 4

They were losing their son. Mike had refused to enter college, stopped church attendance, and found a menial job at a ski resort so he could be a "ski bum." "It's MY life," he said, "and I'm not spending it the way YOU want me to." Clive and Shirley reached out to save him but he slipped away to a collection of bad habits, moving in worse directions. His parents prayed. It was all they could do.

Eventually, Clive and Shirley turned back to the plans they'd made for themselves, which included a mission. They did the paperwork, received their call, and entered the Senior Missionary Training Center. "I worried about leaving Mike," Shirley said, "but on the other hand I thought that our being in the mission field might be the best thing for him. It was definitely a concern, nonetheless."

Clive and Shirley enthusiastically entered a foreign humanitarian mission. Within days, they'd cleaned up an old building that hadn't been swept for years so a school could be established. They jumped into teaching assignments, spent hours developing visual aids, and traveled to small communities in the area. But six months into the mission, Shirley experienced unexplained dizziness. The Country Director transferred the couple to a large city with approved medical facilities, but a diagnosis couldn't be made. As Clive and Shirley continued with their mission assignments, medical testing brought no light to the problem and Priesthood blessings brought no relief. Soon, Shirley needed a cane for balance. The Mission President watched with concern. Shirley insisted she'd get over it, but she didn't. Finally, the Mission President took Shirley by the hand and told her of his decision to send the couple home. Amid protests and tears, arrangements were made and the couple was in their own hometown within the week, devastated and confused. Their willingness to serve a mission had been sincere, yet their sacrifice seemed unacceptable. What went wrong?

Mike hurried home to be with his mother. Her mysterious illness worried him and he stayed to support, encourage, and help out. He started a few college classes and picked up a part-time job. In a surprise move, he quietly paid tithing on his first paycheck, even though he didn't attend church. It was his bargain with God for his mother's sake and he continued to send monthly tithing.

Then, in a series of miraculous coincidences, Mike ran into a high school sweetheart who turned out to be the girl of his dreams. They talked about marriage...temple marriage.

Mike asked Clive to arrange an appointment with the bishop, who walked Mike through the repentance process and right into the temple for his endowment. On the night of his temple experience, Shirley turned to Clive and said, "Look at Mike! He's glowing!" The next week Clive, who had been called to the temple presidency, sealed Mike and his sweetheart for eternity. "If my mother had not come home from her mission," Mike told his Stake President, "I would not be here today!"

Shirley felt a huge burden lift from her heart. "I'm so grateful to Heavenly Father for letting me know I completed the mission He sent me to do. It wasn't the same mission I thought I was to do, but it was so much better." All the questions were answered.

LENGTHEN YOUR SHUFFLE

"Therefore, care not for the body, neither the life of the body; but care for the soul, and for the life of the soul. And seek the face of the Lord always, that in patience ye may possess your soul, and ye shall have eternal life."

D&C 101:37-38

It was World War II and young Doug Jenks found himself in the middle of the Battle of the Bulge. When the fighting finished, Doug was left wounded on the field. Nobody found him, nobody called for help. That night the weather turned mean. Warm blood from his wounds leaked out to solidify on the ground. Finally, his feet froze. When medics finally found him, his feet had to be partially amputated. Doug went home.

Life moves forward and Doug lived forward, like all of us. He wore specially constructed shoes with heavy toes to help his balance. He married, had a family, built a career, and watched his skin wrinkle and his hair turn gray. Then, at the age of 74, he and his wife, Beverly, were called to Thailand to teach English. They developed a program that used singing and dancing and Doug joined in without excuses. He stood in front of his adult students in his special shoes and did the Alphabet Cheer:

"Gimme an A," he shouted.

"...A..." the teachers chorused.

"Gimme a B," he added.

"...B..." they yelled enthusiastically.

49

"Gimme an A,B,C,D,E,F,G..."

While Doug flailed his arms around, his cute little wife did a cheerleader routine. The cheer, with variations, is still in use as a teaching device.

The point is this: Doug had amputated feet whether he stayed home or went on the mission. So he went on the mission.

⚜

Phil and Betty Camps were asked to help with the English program in Thailand. Betty had such severe arthritis she could only sit and smile as her husband taught. They constructed board games such as concentration, bingo, lotto, and fish. Name it and they had it, all handmade for forty students to play at the same time. The games, with their language applications, spread across the country. A year later the Church asked the Camps to take their English games to a school in Nepal. Betty, moving carefully to avoid her arthritis pain, smiled broadly as they boarded the plane for their next adventure.

The point is this: Betty had arthritis whether she stayed home or went on a mission. So she went on the mission.

⚜

In a letter from the Palmyra mission, written by a couple serving in 2002, wrinkled missionaries were discussed.

"The couple missionaries are so valuable! They really are worth their weight in gold. They're very old but talented people: carpenters, electricians, builders. One of the physical facilities men said they figured the couples were worth about a million dollars per mission for the time they spend. They're not here because they survived without any health problems. Most of the men, it seems, have hearing aids. One man was a retired judge who had a hip replacement, then hit his head when he fell down some stairs and was in a coma for months. He thought he'd never speak again, let alone walk. But he and his wife are here and they're great! His short term memory is lacking sometimes, but whose isn't? He walks with a cane but, hey, he's out here doin' it. One of our couples sold everything they have and have served on six consecutive missions, from Fiji to Australia, really great people!"

Church leaders are fully aware of the challenges age brings. President McKay once tripped on his way to the Conference stand. A gasp from the audience brought a smile to his face as he explained, "It's a terrible thing to get old, but it's better than the alternative!" President Hinckley spoke from experience when he said, "The golden years are laced with lead!" With this understanding, why are the leaders requesting older members of the church to donate precious years? Because, even though the lead portion becomes a heavy burden, the gold is forty-four karat and well worth the trouble.

If you've survived to a respectable old age, in spite of hearing aids and hip replacements, you've never been more valuable. Come join the work. Bring your own oxygen.

JUST FARM FOLKS

"Art thou a brother or brethren? I salute you in the name of the Lord Jesus Christ, in token or remembrance of the everlasting covenant, in which covenant I receive you to fellowship."

D&C 88:133

Brother and Sister Brown were a plain, homely, unspectacular Idaho farm couple who showed up in a metropolitan American city around 1984. They stood in the church foyer and looked around, determined to make a difference.

"Hello, we're the Browns, your Ward's new missionary couple and are we ever glad to meet you!" They walked around the chapel giving everyone the same glad-hand treatment, grinning like fools and acting like everyone's long-lost best friend. The Ward members were a little twitchy.

You see, the city was not a warm and friendly place. Its citizens in general had a suspicious glance, and a chip on their shoulder, and no wonder. If you said a friendly hello to a stranger on the street, he might follow you home, rob your house, and phone you all year with improper suggestions. So people in the big city didn't greet strangers with grins and cries of welcome, even at church.

Take Lorie for example. "The first week I lived here," she said, "I answered the phone cheerfully and gave my name to the friendly male caller when he asked it. The voice on the other end changed suddenly to one of menace. 'Hello Lorie. Are you ready to die? I'm watching you through your window and I am going to kill you.'" So it's quite understandable that, after fifteen years in the city, Lorie had adopted an attitude of suspicion toward people who were too friendly. People like Brother and Sister Brown. "Man," she thought, "what's wrong with them? What are they after?"

The Browns spent every week visiting families who had dropped out of activity years before and started bringing some of them back to church. They didn't necessarily give them any discussions. Mostly what they offered was unfeigned friendship and love...love in a city ruled by mistrust and suspicion. "So they were weird," Lorie said. "It was a very pleasant weird. Sort of the way things had been at home in Utah thirty years ago."

As the weeks went by, Lorie looked forward to these hyper-friendly people. They remembered her name, were thrilled to see her, and seemed sincere about the state of her health and happiness.

"I wasn't the only one so affected," she explained. "People in our ward started being more open and friendly—first with the Browns, then with each other. It felt good! And it was nice to meet all the former inactives who were charmed back by the magic of nothing but pure, loving, genuine friendliness. I wanted to be just like the Browns someday."

The Browns worked their magic for a whole year. There was a pit of emptiness in the ward when they returned to their Idaho farm. It was easy to see what a difference they had made in the attitude of the whole congregation.

Lorie is a senior missionary in Fiji now, working in the office during the day, teaching classes at a church school one evening a week, and doing "splits" with the young missionaries. "I learned how to be a GOOD wrinkled missionary from that dear couple who were assigned to my ward twenty years ago," she said.

The Browns: Education? Nothing to speak of. Deep philosophical discussions in Gospel Doctrine class? Nope. Good looks and charisma? Hardly. Just wrinkled missionaries with very loving hearts who were not afraid to show it.

GET THEE BEHIND ME...

"Satan thinketh to overpower your testimony...that the work may not come forth in this generation."

D&C 10:33

Duane and Jean lived in paradise, a home on a lake, their own Walden Pond. With a fishing boat in their backyard and an RV parked nicely at the side, they were ready to tackle a well-earned retirement. Then came the big Call. Would they set up an Employment Center in the Philippines? Even though they hadn't put in papers for a mission, they accepted the assignment and began battening the hatches in preparation for leaving paradise.

The boat was brought to high ground and covered, neighbors were willing to watch the house, the RV was placed in a storage center and it seemed that everything was ready. But, as First Thessalonians 2:18 says, "... Satan hindered us."

A call from their daughter announced that her husband had lost his job and the situation was serious. Duane and Jean discussed the irony of leaving their out-of-work family so they could go to the Philippines and help strangers get jobs. With their mission resolve already wavering, they received another blow. Their son called to advise them that he and his wife were talking about divorce. Leaving now seemed pure folly. If ever a child needed them, it was a son on the verge of divorce. Duane and Jean searched the scriptures.

> *"There hath no temptation taken you but such as is common to man: but God is faithful, who will not suffer you to be tempted above that ye are able; but will with the temptation also make a way to escape, that ye may be able to bear it."*
>
> 1 Corinthians 10:13

The family decided the mission call should be completed. But Satan has had eons of practice and is very good at what he does. The night before Duane and Jean were scheduled to leave, they received more bad news, their RV had been vandalized.

They repaired what could be repaired, locked what could be locked, then looked at each other and shrugged. The next morning, the couple picked up their bags and, with faces toward The Son, simply left.

While their plane was still in the air, their out-of-work kids found another job. By the time they landed in the Philippines their son and his wife were in process of reconciling.

The mission in the Philippines was such a positive experience that they answered another call as Country Directors in Thailand. Then, in proof of their faithfulness, they left their private paradise again to live in Salt Lake City and direct humanitarian missions worldwide.

"Blessed is the man that endureth temptation: for when he is tried, he shall receive the crown of life, which the Lord hath promised to them that love him." James 1:12

Paradise can wait.

ROMANCING THE E-MAIL

"As every man hath received the gift, even so minister the same one to another, as good stewards of the manifold grace of God."

1 Peter 4:10

Etta planned missions with her husband. They talked about it. They agreed on it. But life happens while you're planning something else, and God took Etta's husband to the Spirit World on a mission of his own. So 64-year-old Etta rearranged her plans and went on their mission as a single sister.

It was a wonderful experience, two women on the adventure of a lifetime, seeing a part of the world most people don't even think about, doing things that bring confidence...appreciated and respected in spite of sagging arms, drooping jowls, and widening waists. Other cultures across the world respect age and the wisdom that comes with it. Etta's spirit soared.

Wrinkled missionaries are allowed, even encouraged, to have e-mail. It's one of the perks of age and allows instant communication with the folks back home. Among Etta's friends were a couple she and her husband had dearly loved. They'd shared laughter and tears and dinners over half a lifetime. The wife had suffered an extended illness and her situation became terminal while Etta was at the MTC. Before she died she asked that Etta keep in touch with Frank, her husband. When Etta arrived at her area of service, she sent words of consolation, understanding, and comfort to Frank. She understood his pain. They continued writing.

Several months later, Frank sent an e-mail that went something like this:

"Dear Etta. I wanted to spend my twilight years on missions and now that opportunity is denied me unless I remarry. But there's no one here who seems interested in spending time traipsing around the world in service to the Church. You've already proven your desire to serve, we've been friends for many years so we wouldn't have to waste time getting to know each other, I already love you as the wonderful person you are, would you consider marrying me? Don't say no yet. Think about it.

Love, Frank."

Shock.

Denial.

Surely she'd read it wrong.

She hadn't.

It took a long time to say *"This is so sudden"* and *"Give me time to think about it"*

Frank wrote back.

"I'm sure I can find a nice lady here who would be willing to serve the Lord by my side, but I'd prefer you. I already love you. I can give you a little time to think about it, but not much. I'm getting older as we speak. Time's wasting.

Love, Frank."

Etta prayed and pondered...and blushed. A marriage proposal at her age! The other single sister missionaries reverted to girlhood as they advised, counseled, and listened to concerns. "What would my husband and Frank's wife think?" Etta said. "They might believe we'd always had a little affair going on between us. They might..."

"They might be thrilled to death!" said a little lady from Canada. Then, realizing what she'd said she put her face in her hands. "Oh, I'm sorry! I didn't mean it that way! Oh, my goodness, pardon that pun." Laughter is a good thing and clears brain cells. Etta accepted Frank's proposal of marriage.

A ring. There had to be an engagement ring and (practical as always) Frank e-mailed the suggestion that she visit a jeweler there ,on the other side of the world, and choose her own. Giggling like schoolgirls, the sisters of the mission tumbled into taxis and went to a wholesale outlet named "Johnny's Gems" where they helped Etta choose the biggest, flashiest, best bargain diamond ring in the store. They bent their heads together to inspect each ring and give opinions. From a fluffy cloud of hair in shades of white and gray came a chorus of "ooooo's" and "ahhhhh's" until the perfect match was found. Etta's next e-mail to Frank said, "Have ring. Send money."

Etta finished her mission and went home to Frank, nervous but happy. They visited the graves of their eternal companions, then married in a temple ceremony for time. A few months later, they were in Bangkok, Thailand. They sent lots of e-mails to friends and family back home.

THE GUARANTEES

There aren't any.

Your grandchildren will grow older and they'll do it without you. You could come home and find your house destroyed and your finances in a mess. Relatives could have died and you weren't with them when they passed to the other side. Children might have divorced. All of it could happen. The trials of life are the same for kings or paupers, young or old, wicked or righteous, me or you, on a mission or not. If we're still breathing, life happens. And sometimes life is nasty. Nevertheless, an apostolic blessing has been given to the mature missionaries of the Church. It is a blessing so beautiful that any sacrifice is worth the gift.

The blessing was given by Elder Jeffrey Holland to the older couples and sisters in Hong Kong in 1999, but the promise extends to all of us who have raised our families, lived our lives, and continue to look for ways to enlarge our souls.

Elder Holland began by directing his remarks to the missionaries as grandparents. "All our lives," he said, "we've prayed for our grandchildren, and now it's their turn to pray for us." He spoke of the heritage we are leaving our families through missionary service and the example we set for them. "You are half a world away from your families," he said, "and doing more for them now than you ever could by staying home."

He left an apostolic blessing, saying the blessing would be as true and individual as if he laid his hands on our heads. "Because of you," he proclaimed, "all your children and your children's children will be drawn home; they will choose to come home. Your children and your children's children will call your name blessed. Even on the other side of the veil, you will be entitled to bless your grandchildren for generations to come. God will empower you."

Elder Holland continued to explain, this is the dispensation of the fullness of times. We are so close to history we don't know we're making it. "Virtually everything we do is unprecedented," he said. "No other people in any dispensation have had as great a responsibility. The work is all ours."

The Lord Himself has given promises to those who enter into His work:

"Lift up your heart and rejoice, for the hour of your mission is come...and you shall declare glad tidings of great joy unto this generation. Therefore, thrust in your sickle with all your soul, and your sins are forgiven you, and you shall be laden with sheaves upon your back, for the laborer is worthy of his hire. Wherefore, your family shall live. Behold, verily I say unto you, go from them only for a little time, and declare my word, and I will prepare a place for them."

D&C 1:3-6